MW01073465

To Hal Schulz

To a Friend that "sticks
closer than a brother".
If ever in a "Fox-hole", I
want you there.
God continue to bless
and use you.

KICK THE TIRES
AND LIGHT THE FIRES

If any of
you marine
pilots would
buy - I'd give
you boostore
Price

IS

WINEPRESS WP PUBLISHING

Printed in the United States of America
Editorial assistant Joe Harms, son of Vernon Harms.
Illustrations by Randy Zistel.

A note of thanks to a terrific friend, Dr. H. D. Shultz for the use of "Plan of Salvation" in the back of this book.

Packaged by WinePress Publishing, PO Box 1406, Mukilteo, WA 98275. The views expressed or implied in this work do not necessarily reflect those of WinePress Publishing. Ultimate design, content, and editorial accuracy of this work is the responsibility of the author(s).

Unless otherwise noted, Scripture quotations in this book are taken from the Holy Bible, New International Version, Copyright © 1973, 1978, 1984 by the International Bible Society. Used by permission of Zondervan Publishing House. The "NIV" and "New International Version" trademarks are registered in the United States Patent and Trademark Office by International Bible Society.

Verses marked KJV are taken from the King James Version of the Bible.

Verses marked NASB are taken from the New American Standard Bible, © 1960, 1963, 1968, 1971, 1972, 1973, 1975, 1977 by The Lockman Foundation. Used by permission.

Verses marked RSV are taken from the Revised Standard Version of the Bible. Copyright 1946, 1952, 1971 by the Division of Christian Education of the National Council of the Churches of Christ in the U.S.A. Used by permission.

ISBN 1-57921-160-7
Library of Congress
    Catalog Card Number: 98-75111

High Flight

Oh, I have slipped the surly bonds of earth,
And danced the skies on laughter-silvered wings;
Sunward I've climbed, and joined
the tumbling mirth

Of sun-split clouds, and done a hundred things
You have not dreamed of—wheeled
and soared and swung
High in the sunlit silence. Hov'ring there,
I've chased the shouting wind along and flung

My eager craft through footless halls of air . . .
Up, up the long delirious, burning blue
I've topped the windswept heights
with easy grace
Where never lark nor ever eagle flew—

And, while with silent lifting mind I've trod
The high untrespassed sanctity of space,
Put out my hand and touched the face of God.

—John Gillispie Magee Jr.
Royal Canadian Air Force

"Having just returned from a stressful and successful sale of a Lear Jet, Vern Harms reported to Bill's office with the signed contract. A board meeting was in progress and Bill took Vern into the board room and introduced him as "the best salesman he had seen."

—Moya Olsen Lear

"As a former member of the Civil Air Patrol, I can personally attest to its contribution to the nation. The CAP is involved in a range of activities from search and rescue to drug interdiction missions, and I believe it grooms America's youth by challenging them with real world situations and opportunities. . . . I salute the CAP and recognize their vital contribution to our great nation."

—General Michael E. Ryan
Chief of Staff
United States Air Force

Contents

CONTENTS

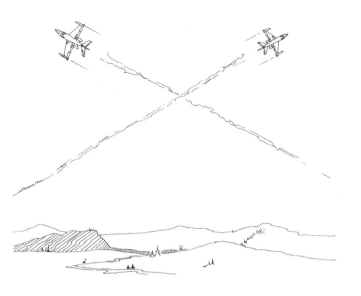

Crossroads and Contrails

(Some of these articles first appeared, although
in a different form, in the *Cap News* under the
title "Crossroads to Contrails.")

1 Crossroads—As we take our journey through
life, we will encounter many crossroads. They
will become obstacles or opportunities. When
tragedy strikes, whether in your own life or in
the lives of family or friends, or when joys come,
when you just need to talk to someone, call a chaplain, pastor, or trusted Christian friend. A recent article in *USA Today* was headlined, "Few would turn
to clergy for help if they were dying." It continued:

"Many Americans want spiritual comfort in their final days, but only one-third think clergy would be very helpful in providing it, shows a new Gallup Institute poll. Clergymen are seen as ministers of religion—boxed in by creeds and dogmas, says theological historian Robert Webber of Wheaton (Ill.) College. But most people don't want religion, they want spirituality."

Most of the chaplains and ministers with whom I have worked through the years are worthy of your confidence, and they will share Scripture and Christ with you when you are in need. As we cross through turbulent skies and are tossed with the storms of life—let's do it together. We may not and do not have all of the answers, but we have a Friend to whom we can guide you and pray together to ease your burden as we cross life's crossroads. "A man of many companions may come to ruin, but there is a friend who sticks closer than a brother" (Prov. 18:24). For me that Friend is Christ. "It is God who arms me with strength and makes my way perfect. He makes my feet like the feet of a deer; he enables me to stand on the heights" (2 Sam. 22:33–34). I hope this devotional book will help you make the right turn toward God when next you are confronted with a crossroads.

Contrails—Looking down from the cockpit of a jet at 41,000 feet and seeing the contrail on the clouds below for the first time, I realized how much more relaxing it is to be up there above the traffic, both radio and aircraft traffic. It also beats dodging granite clouds (mountains hidden in clouds) and tops of pine trees any day. Is much of my life spent in "low-level" thinking, living, and planning? Do I really set my affections on things above? "Set your affection on things above, not on things on the earth" (Col. 3:2 KJV).

Low-level flying was required on the search missions we used to fly, but in our spiritual lives we might well claim the United States Air Force slogan, "Aim high!" Is my life spent on bickering about nonessentials, trivia, etc., rather than on the true mission as directed by those whom I serve? "Let Thy salvation, O God, set me up on high" (Ps. 69:29b KJV). Every pilot I know loves to fly high. It has been said, "The two most useless things to a pilot are the sky above and the runway that is behind you."

So—from now on—when you come to a *crossroads* in your life, take the high road and blaze a *contrail*. Others will notice and be encouraged by your steady walk with the Lord. "For you have delivered me from death and my feet from stumbling, that I may walk before God in the light of life" (Ps. 56:13). If, in your journey through life, the ministerial profession has failed you in some way, perhaps you can come to the Godly laity and find peace. Will you be that person—clergy or laity—to whom searchers can come? You can be!

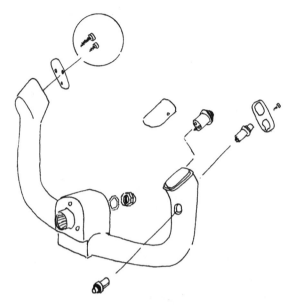

Do It Right the First Time – You May Save a Life

2 Is your journey through life really a life-or-death matter? It really is! An assembly line job that requires putting short screws into an electrical inspection plate on the control column could seem unimportant to some. But that task became an important one when, one sunny morning, another pilot and I were test-flying a Lear Jet out of Wichita, Kansas, in Boot Hill Test Area A & B. After testing various items at altitudes (flight levels) of 10,000, 20,000, 30,000, and 40,000 feet, we were relaxing at 41,000 feet and drinking a can of pop cooled on the unupholstered clamshell door, frosty from the OAT (outside air temperature) of 65+ degrees below zero. Upon beginning our descent, we suddenly realized we had a runaway nose-down elevator trim. Testing the override switch, we found it had no effect. All the way back to Wichita, both of us had to pull back on the yoke with all our strength to keep the nose from going down and taking us into a charred crater with our bodies in the middle. We prayed that the cables would not break on the nonboosted control system.

The Bible has something to say about doing our work in a professional and proper way: "Whoever can be trusted with very little can also be trusted with much, and whoever is dishonest with very little will also be dishonest with much" (Luke 16:10).

How important is your seemingly minor task in life? It may make a world of difference if you don't perform it properly. There is no minor task for any of us. We are God's handiwork—the zenith of His creation and the highest work of His hands. "Whatever your hand finds to do, do it with all your might, for in the grave, where you are going, there is neither working nor planning nor knowledge nor wisdom" (Eccles. 9:10).

In our service to God, country, and fellow men, let us act with a feeling of responsibility. An usher's approach can ruin or augment the message on

Sunday morning. A human life may not always be in jeopardy, but one's personal actions will always affect others in one's home, place of work, or at play—be it good or bad. Let's all aim high and leave a contrail of excellence. "Now it is *required* that those who have been given a trust must prove faithful" (1 Cor. 4:2 emphasis added). There are those who say God can't and doesn't guide us in the small details of life. Doesn't He? Listen to Matthew 10:29–31: "Are not two sparrows sold for a penny? Yet not one of them will fall to the ground apart from the will of your Father. And even the very hairs of your head are all numbered. So don't be afraid; you are worth more than many sparrows."

Later we learned that the problem occurred because someone on the assembly line had put a longer screw into a plate on the control column, thus piercing the wire cover.

"God bless and enable each of us to do our jobs with integrity" is my prayer.

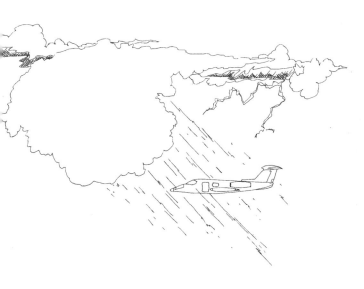

Battered by Storms?
Enter God's Ark

3 Fuselage! Did you ever wonder about the real purpose of the fuselage? We all know the importance of wings, spoilers, ailerons, empennage (tail assembly of the aircraft), and other control surfaces. But why does an aircraft have a fuselage? Is it only to keep the power plant, wings, and tail together? That could be accomplished with a single lightweight "I" beam, or some type of smaller-than-usual monocoque framework. In the early stages of flight, the primary function of the fuselage was for the protection of the pilot from the elements. More recently it has also become a shelter for exotic instruments and controls. When flying in ice or at temperatures of minus 65 degrees, aren't you glad someone designed a comfortable fuselage with a warm cockpit?

The ark! In similar manner, God told Noah to build an ark to protect his own family and also ensure the continuation of His created world. "The LORD then said to Noah, 'Go into the ark, you and your whole family, because I have found you righteous in this generation. . . Seven days from now I will send rain on the earth for forty days and forty nights, and I will wipe from the face of the earth every living creature I have made.' *And Noah did all that the LORD commanded him*" (Genesis 7:1, 4–5). From many centuries back, man has asked for God's protection and blessing when going into battle or on hazardous exercises. Our troops during Desert Storm, as in other past conflicts, paused to ask chaplains of many different faiths to pray for their protection. "The eternal God is thy refuge and underneath are the everlasting arms" (Deut. 33:27). As you have been launched into another new day, why not ask God to be your ark, your "fuselage," to protect you not only from physical danger but also from lack of faith and the threat of decaying morals that have so infiltrated our society? "Hear my cry, O God; listen to my prayer. From the ends of the earth I call to you, I call as my heart grows faint; lead me to the rock that is higher than I. For you have been my refuge, a strong tower against the foe" (Ps. 61:1–3).

"If he (God) . . . did not spare the ancient world when he brought the flood on its ungodly people, but protected Noah, a preacher of righteousness, and seven others . . . if this is so, then the Lord knows how to rescue godly men from trials and to hold the unrighteous for the day of judgment, while continuing their punishment" (2 Peter 2:5, 9). Have you entered God's ark of salvation? "For in the days before the flood, people were eating and drinking, marrying and giving in marriage, up to the day Noah entered the ark; and they knew nothing about what would happen until the flood came and took them all away. That is how it will be at the coming of the Son of Man. Two men will be in the field; one will be taken and the other left. Two women will be grinding with a hand mill; one will be taken and the other left. Therefore keep watch, because you do not know on what day your Lord will come" (Matt. 24:38–42).

My prayer is that each of you will find God a source of protection and help, and your spiritual leaders an avenue of present-day and eternal guidance. "Be merciful unto me, O God, be merciful unto me; for my soul trusteth in thee: yea, in the shadow of thy wings will I make my refuge, until these calamities be [passed by]" (Ps. 57:1 KJV).

"By faith Noah, when warned about things not yet seen, in holy fear built an ark to save his family. By his faith he condemned the world and became heir of the righteousness that comes by faith." (Heb. 11:7)

If you are not sure of your own relationship to God, turn to the last pages in this book for guidance.

What Will Splatter–You, the Chicken, or the Shield?

4 I stood beside Bill Lear as he fired a .38-caliber revolver directly at the windshield of our jet aircraft nose section mockup. After repeated firings, not one bullet penetrated the two-piece windshield. Pleased with the results, I now trusted fully in the integrity of that windshield.

The time came for the FAA-monitored tests, in which a pneumatic gun would hurl a four-pound chicken at 300 knots toward various locations on the windshield. Having established trust in our creation, I eagerly volunteered to sit in the cockpit during the test. Calmer heads prevailed, and a Styrofoam dummy took my place.

Bang! The air gun blasted the chicken, and with a puff of feathers the windshield was gone—and with it, the head of the dummy! Had I planted my body in the pilot's seat for the test, the experience would not have been habit-forming. Later a three-piece windshield, a T-bar "chicken splitter" in the middle of the windshield, and additional structure changes remedied the problem.

Are you trusting in something or someone that has not been tested? Be assured that God and His mercy have never failed those who put their trust in Him. "The works of His hands are verity and judgement; all His commandments are sure" (Ps. 111:7 KJV).

In the same way I trusted an untested windshield, perhaps you have trusted something or someone untested, and maybe you've gotten "splattered" a time or two. Why not put your trust in Someone who has been tested again and again and is always found able to stand as a Shield? "For the Lord God is a sun and shield; the Lord will give grace and glory. . . . no good thing will he withhold from them that walk uprightly" (Ps. 84:11 KJV).

Let's all get behind the true and tested Shield and enjoy the peace, protection, and comfort the

Master Designer plans for us. "Do not let your hearts be troubled. Trust in God; trust also in me. In my Father's house are many rooms; if it were not so, I would have told you. I am going there to prepare a place for you" (John 14:1–2).

"ALL IS WELL"

Confidence in Self or God

5 The Midwest non-instrument-rated pilot was flying night VFR (Visual Flight Rules) on top of clouds. He checked en route flight service stations for weather conditions at his destination and along the route of flight. Thinking he had to get his passengers and himself home on time, he continued to climb to remain above the clouds. Soon the gradual symptoms of hypoxia (oxygen lack at high altitude) set in. "Stopwatch Flight Service Sta-

tion, yes, I'm OK. . . . S a a a y a g-g a i n n, p l z z z z." A lack of oxygen due to high altitude flying without proper equipment on board had caused hypoxia. The pilot was, by now, unaware of slurred speech and other impairments. Zep Aero says that the most hazardous feature of hypoxia as it relates to general aviation is its gradual and insidious onset. The fact that it creates a false euphoria and feeling of total well-being is the dangerous aspect of the symptoms. Other related symptoms are impairment of vision and judgment, high self-confidence, disregard for sensory perceptions, poor coordination, drowsiness, dizziness, and personality changes as if intoxicated.

Our Maker has created us body, soul, and spirit. We need to care for and nourish all three. When my relationship with my God is not what it should be, I occasionally have a feeling of false well-being, insensitivity to what is going on around me, a high feeling of self-confidence, etc. At times warnings may come from fellow passengers on life's journey. Do I listen to the small quiet voice of the Holy Spirit? My day is generally bound for either storm or calm according to my time of meditation. "My mouth shall speak of wisdom, and the meditation of my heart shall be of understanding" (Ps. 49:3 KJV). If my head is "up in the clouds" and "spiritual hypoxia" takes over, I may cause both people and plans to perish. We are warned in God's Word that these spiritual conditions can ensnare us. "Who being past feeling have given themselves over unto lasciviousness, to work all uncleanness with greediness. But ye have not so learned Christ" (Eph. 4:19–20 KJV).

After having been told that he had low ceilings, snow, and freezing conditions ahead, the pilot laughingly brushed aside the warning and continued the flight. The next day marked the beginning of our long and futile search over a large, snow-covered area of rough terrain. The aircraft and six victims were found by a rancher the following spring after the snow melted.

"Where no counsel is, the people fall: but in the multitude of counselors there is safety" (Prov. 11:14 KJV).

"We who worship by the Spirit of God, who glory in Christ Jesus, and who put no confidence in the flesh (Phil. 3:3b).

Have you put your trust in Christ as Savior? If you are searching for answers, why not turn to the back of this book and read the section marked *Plan of Salvation?*

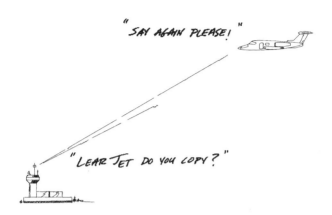

Your Last Instructions
May be . . . Your Last

6 The night was dark, and storm clouds covered the radar screen. What an awful night to totally lose one side of our navigation and communication system. That's right, to further complicate our stressful approach to LaGuardia Airport, New York City, we lost the communication side of our primary nav/com system as we were handed off to New York Center. A night instrument approach to LGA in a storm is bad enough, but when you can't communicate with the control center or the tower, it does get a little lonely. You feel alone and forsaken.

Have you ever felt that God has forsaken you? Is no one talking to you? Let me assure you that His equipment has not failed. He has not left His microphone. "If I rise on the wings of the dawn, if I settle on the far side of the sea, even there your hand will guide me, your right hand will hold me fast. If I say, 'Surely the darkness will hide me and the light become night around me,' even the darkness will not be dark to you; the night will shine like the day, for darkness is as light to you" (Ps. 139:9–12).

Without communication with New York Center, what do you do? First of all, you adjust your transponder to 7700 for a period of one minute. Then you turn the transponder to and remain on 7600 for fifteen minutes or the remainder of the flight. If you are at your approach fix *ahead* of time, establish a holding pattern and begin your approach at the expected approach time given on your clearance. If you arrive at your approach fix on or *after* the expected approach time, go ahead and shoot the approach. The important thing is that you *follow your last instructions.*

"In the past God spoke to our forefathers through the prophets at many times and in various ways, but in these last days he has spoken to us by his Son, whom he appointed heir of all things, and through whom he made the universe" (Heb. 1:1–2).

If God, through His Word, His Spirit, a chaplain, a minister, or a friend, has conveyed instructions to you and you haven't "heard from Him" lately, could it be that you haven't followed His last instructions? Check it out! "But it is good for me to draw near to God: I have put my trust in the Lord God, that I may declare all thy works" (Ps. 73:28 KJV).

(By the way, if you think flying into LaGuardia Airport with no communication is difficult, try to taxi to Butler Aviation with only light signals from the tower.)

A Team Player or a Know-It-All?

7 The United States Air Force Thunderbirds! Just the name, Thunderbirds, will put goose bumps on your skin! How do you become a pilot in this precision flying team? What is required? In an interview with Capt. Jeff Rochelle, the Thunderbirds' left wing, I learned a lot about the requirements. He and Capt. Joe La Marca's entire public affairs staff did a gracious job in hosting me at Nellis AFB, Nevada. "Being a team player is a major

requirement in flying with the team," said Capt. Rochelle. Very quickly I learned that you can't be a lone hotshot pilot and fill a slot on the team.

"With so many pilots to choose from, how did you get selected for flying with the Thunderbirds?" I asked. His response, which should be the goal of each one of us in our duty station, was that he always did the best possible job in whatever task was expected of him. Helping and serving others as a team member is what it's all about. Israel won the battle as long as Moses had his arms raised. How long can you hold your arms up unsupported? Moses dropped his arms and others suffered. We find some real teamwork in the account in Exodus: "As long as Moses held up his hands, the Israelites were winning, but whenever he lowered his hands, the Amalekites were winning. When Moses' hands grew tired, they took a stone and put it under him and he sat on it. Aaron and Hur held his hands up—on one side, one on the other—so that his hands remained steady till sunset. So Joshua overcame the Amalekite army with the sword" (Exod. 17:11–13).

Moses would have been proud of the Thunderbirds! We all are! Is God proud of the way we are helping our fellow members of the body of Christ? Can your employer be proud of the way you support the program he has asked you to perform, and do you carry out his plans? Would each of us want a staff member who is just as much a team player as we are on the staff of our own immediate boss/

commander? "Two are better than one, because they have a good return for their work: If one falls down, his friend can help him up. But pity the man who falls and has no one to help him up!" (Ecc. 4:9–10).

I have yet to see a team that is more supportive of each other than the Thunderbirds, our Ambassadors in Blue. They are a model for both us as pilots and those of us who do the important job of manning the ground support teams.

The next time you see a need in your unit/group, think about Aaron and Hur. You read a lot about Moses, but in this instance, these two men made him a victorious commander. Think about it!

" MY SPIRITUAL COURSE "

Absolutes in the Flight of Life

It was Christmas Day and a traffic fatality needed to be flown from one Midwest city to another. I was elected to do it. Checking the weather, renting an airplane, and filing a flight plan seemed very routine. Taking my eldest son along for company, I embarked on the trip. Several hundred miles later we began encountering unreported freezing rain. Since this was not in the forecast, I continued on and thought mistakenly that it would soon abate. I should have turned around immediately and used alternative transportation methods. Instead I continued to the next city and picked up so much ice that full throttle was required to maintain flying speed. The actual creaking of the aircraft as I turned on a shallow final reminded me that I had not followed some absolute standards in my flight. Don't fly without de-ice equipment in known icing conditions! I nearly self-destructed! I thank God for the retired United States Air Force instructor who years ago drilled into my student brain how to deal with heavy ice—full speed until you are over the runway, then—and only then—chop your power.

In an aircraft, thrust must overcome drag and lift must overcome gravity, or the plane will not fly. Ice on the wings that disturbs the smooth flow of air or causes the aircraft to be too heavy has doomed many a flight. These serve as fatal examples of violating some simple absolutes.

Just as there are absolute standards for flight, God has established absolute standards for life. Will we as a nation self-destruct if we fail to adhere to basic moral principles? Can we continue to ignore God's absolutes without a shocking national tragedy?

"He has showed you, O man, what is good. And what does the LORD require of you? To act justly and to love mercy and to walk humbly with your God." (Micah 6:8)

Absolute honesty would serve as a great starting point in making our spiritual life "fly high." When I promise to do a task, can people consider it done? Are my reports totally honest, or do I give people what they want to read? Do I face God's Word with an open and honest heart?

Absolute purity demands proper motives, thoughts, and intentions. Are "hidden agendas" preventing people from totally trusting me or supporting my plans?

Absolute unselfishness would certainly make all Christian groups into one cohesive organization. Someone has said that more great things would be done if no one cared who got the credit. Has too great an emphasis on denominational differences robbed us of being an effective force against evil? I wonder what kind of scoreboard God uses to tally up who has the most members. I doubt if He has such a scoreboard!

Absolute love will be a sure thing if we follow the preceding suggestions. It is hard to learn to separate someone's undesirable deed from that individual. I know of no way to do it other than to ask God for His love and then apply it to others.

Airline captains follow absolutes in their flight operations. May God grant us the will to follow His absolutes in our spiritual "flight operations."

("Absolutes" borrowed from *Moral Rearmament*)

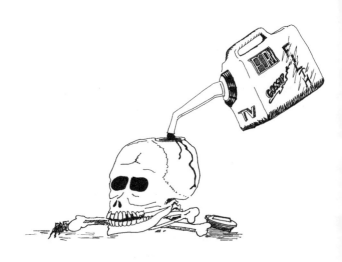

You Are What You Ingest

9 Fuel contamination or fuel exhaustion may both result in either partial or total loss of power. Some of us, the fortunate ones, have survived emergency landings, even though we were not as cautious as we should have been.

My question is—are we as a nation suffering from spiritual fuel contamination or starvation? A full load of fuel in the tanks appears to meet the needs of the reciprocal or jet engine. But do you know the source of the fuel? Were contaminants kept out of the supply storage units? Was ample time allowed for the fuel to settle so that any water would be exhausted when the sump was drained?

Civil Air Patrol cadets, during my teaching of Moral Leadership sessions, have expressed concern about what appears on radio, television, and the printed page. Does one's mind become contaminated by feeding on an endless chain of violence, pornography, and filthy language? Will what enters the mind via any of the senses affect character, attitudes, or spiritual strength or weakness? "Keep your heart with all vigilance, for from it flow the springs of life" (Prov. 4:23 RSV). Studies prove that what our mind ingests may totally or at least partially be what we become. Prison inmates testify they merely reenacted a television show and thus committed their crime. Someone has said that we are what we read.

"Thy word have I hid in mine heart, that I might not sin against thee" (Ps. 119:11 KJV). What a great way to keep one's thoughts and actions headed in the right direction. The Book on which our forefathers established our freedoms will still work to keep us strong and healthy as a nation.

America is a mighty nation, and Desert Storm and other conflicts revealed our ability to unite and fight. Our citizens in uniform proudly obeyed their commanders. Many renewed their individual spiritual commitments, and others made first-time decisions. Chaplains were kept busy! I wonder if our might as a nation will be sustained.

In our own worship places or workplaces, will the spiritual power to perform be there when we are called on to act? I hope and pray that it will be. "From heaven the LORD looks down and sees all mankind; from his dwelling place he watches all who live on earth—he who forms the hearts of all, who considers everything they do. No king is saved by the size of his army; no warrior escapes by his great strength. A horse [fighter jet] is a vain hope for deliverance; despite all its great strength it cannot save. But the eyes of the LORD are on those who fear him, on those whose hope is in his unfailing love" (Ps. 33:13–18).

May I offer a personal challenge to each reader? Ingest only what you want to become.

"For out of the overflow of the heart the mouth speaks. The good man brings good things out of the good stored up in him, and the evil man brings evil things out of the evil stored up in him. But I tell you that men will have to give account on the day of judgment for every careless word they have spoken. For by your words you will be acquitted, and by your words you will be condemned." (Matt. 12:34b–37)

Internal Power or "Jump Start" Required?

10 Having been gone from our home for a while this spring, I went to start my four-wheel-drive vehicle. Remembering that a year ago I had put in a new "live easy" battery, I turned the key with confidence. Nothing! Utterly disgusted, I connected my small battery charger. It wouldn't even *take* a charge! As a final resort I connected my jumper cables to the other car and "jump started" it. "Jump starting" has become a familiar term in recent years. Our United States economy is at times "jump started," and once again we recover from a recession.

If you run across someone who needs a boost, either spiritually or materially, remember God's solution to the problem. "Do not withhold good from those who deserve it, when it is in your power to act. Do not say to your neighbor, 'Come back later; I'll give it tomorrow'—when you now have it with you" (Prov. 3:27–28). I was discussing this topic with a friend recently, and we agreed that at times we must follow principles and do good to people even if our good deeds are not appreciated.

Driving around Sunriver to do several errands, I left my car running to charge the battery. A half mile from home I tested the battery power by turning on the lights. Instant death! Too proud to call my wife to come and *again* "jump start" me, I walked across a golf course, through backyards, and past barking dogs (here I did put on my afterburners) to get home.

How often in my chaplain or pilot duties have I failed to ask God and others for help? Maybe too proud? Have you ever tried, when you felt alone in your family or other duties, to pause just one moment and ask God for power and insight to make the right decision? God is in the business of "jump starting" His children. "But the salvation of the righteous is of the Lord, he is their strength in the time of trouble. And the Lord shall help them, and deliver them; he shall deliver them from the wicked, and save them, because they trust in him" (Ps. 37:39–40 KJV).

The local dealer in our city gave me a new battery at no charge (no pun intended). Could it be that some of us need a new battery? Have you ever asked God to take a vital and daily part in the direction of your life and those of others around you? While agonizing with a dead battery on our village street, I thought, "Thank God I'm not on a Southern California freeway or the New Jersey Turnpike; what a mess I'd make for other travelers." I still, as always, carry a set of jumper cables in my car, even though I have not used them for a while. I want to be ready to help a pilgrim on his journey or be helped during times when I am low on power. My new battery solved a lot of frustrations, time delays, and bother to both me and others. As I travel on my spiritual journey and you see me stalled in traffic, I'd surely appreciate a "boost" . . . wouldn't you?

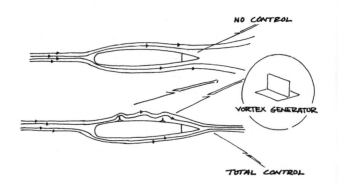

NO CONTROL

VORTEX GENERATOR

TOTAL CONTROL

Trust God–Turbulence Keeps Us in Line

11 Have you ever been asked, "Does that aircraft have a vortex generator?" Before you replied, you may have wondered: "Does a vortex generator generate AC or DC current? Is it belt or gear-driven?" No, none of the above! Shaped like an inverted *T*, the vortex generator is attached to the wing or tail surface of some high-performance aircraft. It actually generates a vortex or small area of turbulence. When a wing passes through the air at high speed, the wind has a tendency to separate from the aileron and other control surfaces, thus rendering control ineffective. It is possible for the aircraft to then go into such vibrations that it will self-destruct, literally vibrate till it breaks up.

Talk about turbulence in life—a USAF airman had a vortex-generator–like experience. Rushing to the airport to catch his plane for his home base, he had a tire blow out on his car. *Oh, no,* he thought, *I'll be AWOL.*

Upon late arrival at the terminal, the young airman learned that his already departed commercial airliner had crashed with no survivors. What at first appeared to be an unhappy experience had now proved to be a life-saving "vortex generator." The flat tire had saved his life.

As God plans and directs our lives, He allows design placement of vortex generators much like the aircraft manufacturer. And as the Pilot of our lives, God can then maintain control. By disturbing the airflow in the wind stream, the vortex generator keeps the surface wind in touch with the control surfaces and avoids an out-of-control destructive situation at high speeds. Wind tunnel tests and actual flight with pieces of yarn on the skin of the aircraft allow photographic data to ensure proper placement of the vortex generators. Am I ever glad that the hand of my Creator is in charge as He allows apparent disturbances to guide my journey through life. "But he knows the way that I take; when he has tested me, I will come forth as gold" (Job 23:10). "No discipline seems pleasant at the time, but painful. Later on, however, it produces a harvest of righteousness and peace for those who have been trained by it" (Heb. 12:11).

Have you ever thanked God for some of the vortexes He has allowed to come your way? It is hard to do so during the "turbulence" unless you fully trust Him for the outcome. "Before I was afflicted I went astray, but now have I kept thy word" (Ps. 119:67 KJV).

Are You Navigating on the Right Station?

12 Many events have changed our world and society as a whole. Neither will ever be the same! Several large nations and one superpower have been fragmented into small countries. Earthquakes, hurricanes, tidal waves, floods, riots, young lives snuffed out in classroom shootings, and other tragedies have left all of us wondering where to turn for strength and stability. Military drawdowns have created financial and domestic instability. Could God, our Creator, now be able to use these changing events to focus our eyes on Him and His Word? "It is better to trust in the Lord than to put confidence in man. It is better to trust in the Lord than to put confidence in princes" (Ps. 118:8–9 KJV).

In this book I have tried to encourage loyalty; responsibility in the home and workplace; cooperation with our peers and authorities; and moral absolutes like perfect honesty, purity, unselfishness, and love. Have we in this nation of freedom and wealth— with renewed purpose—marked our *crossroads* and made higher *contrails?*

We need to face the fact that some of the abovementioned events have left a void in our purpose and direction as we, the United States, face the future. We now have no "super enemy" from without, but can "the enemy from within," as a past president has stated, now destroy us? Is there now a tremendous vacuum that can cause us to drift aimlessly? I still laugh at the flight student from whom I took both the electrical navigation aids and flight chart and asked him to point out landmarks as to where he was located. "I don't really know, but we are making good time," was his reply. Scientific knowledge is increasing at such a rapid rate that chart makers can't keep up with making new classroom charts. We are moving at an unprecedented pace—but where to? Can superb technology and a strong economy save us from moral doom? I don't think so. Can strong nuclear alliances and trade agreements make us a bastion of moral strength? Hardly! "Woe to those who go down to Egypt for help, who rely on horses, who trust in the multitude of their chariots and in the great strength of their horsemen, but do not look to the Holy One of Israel, or seek help from the LORD" (Isa. 31:1).

Some blame the government for our loss of integrity and other moral woes. That is a wrong approach, since *we are the government.* David, the mighty warrior, said to God that he, David, was the one who had failed God. We must each ask ourselves, "If our nation were only as strong and purposeful as I am, where would we be?"

Proper navigation demands listening to the Divine Controller. Isaiah 30:21 says "Whether you turn to the right or to the left, your ears will hear a voice behind you, saying, 'This is the way, walk (fly) in it.'"

What is your personal aim on life's journey? Are you "homed in" on the standards of God's Word?

"HEY— HA.HA, DID YOU HEAR THE ONE ABOUT THE . . . . "

Get Back to the Basics

Flying in a fabric-covered tail dragger and learning the now long-forgotten "A" and "N" signal seems like a dream or maybe even a nightmare. Trying to hear the signal fading in and out above the sometimes unkind voice of my instructor made flying into the cone of silence (the loss of all signals when you "arrive" over the radio station) an unnerving experience. During these early hours of flying under the hood, I had many experiences with vertigo. That's when you feel as if you're flying straight and level, but you may in fact be in a graveyard spiral. If uncorrected, I guarantee this won't be habit-forming!

When you react to feelings rather than to the instrument panel, disaster is just around the corner. Our current philosophy, "If it feels good, do it," will not bring lasting security. God's people, Israel, went through a period when they didn't listen to God or to their kings, and we are told: "In those days there was no king in Israel: every man did that which was right in his own eyes" (Judg. 21:25 KJV). God's Word can keep us flying in a controlled manner, just like the instruments in the panel of an aircraft. And it makes no difference how long you've been flying; you can't rely on your feelings and live to be an old pilot.

Flying from Atlanta to Wichita, I remembered that one of our jets was at the Arkansas City Airport with a new engine change and needed to be picked up. After landing and doing a brief preflight, the other crew left, and I "lit the fires" and lined up on the runway. Since it was a clear night, with VFR conditions, I poured the jet fuel to the engines and away I went—without doing the usual focusing on the instruments. Within seconds my "homesick angel" had me heaven-bound, and there was nothing outside the windshield but black sky. I had hit the proverbial "inkwell," the black hole from which many have not recovered.

After a few seconds of pure terror (some of you know what I mean), I focused on the eight ball and remembered that I had not taken the instrument panel as something I needed for a short VFR flight. I never did that again! I had forgotten that under all circumstances, you follow the manual. I could not get by with doing what was right in my own eyes.

Are we in America following God's manual? He has given us a wealth of guidelines (instruments) for use in our lives. In a world of shifting political rhetoric on "values," let's sharpen up on flying "blind" by never taking our eyes off of the instruments and the Master Controller. "Thou dost guide me with thy counsel, and afterward thou wilt receive me to glory" (Ps. 73:24 RSV).

I remembered what happened during my initial instrument training (it really never stops). I flew into a military base, and breaking out of the clouds, I saw that immense slab of concrete. Was I ever one proud airplane driver. As you travel your journey through life, I hope you have as much inner joy and peace as I experienced on my first wet-weather instrument approach. Friends, keep climbing on course!

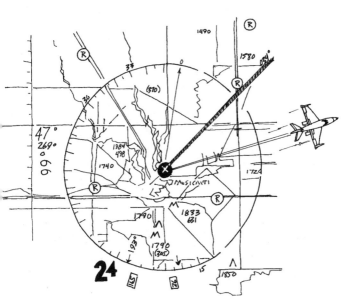

No Kidding, Indy Center—
You Think I'm Off Course?

The political "in" word seems to be "change." At times we can hardly wait for change, and in certain other instances the very thought of change sends shivers down our spines. A wrong change in our income, a downward change in our health, or a change in our job situation may be very frightening. Aren't we glad that our God does not change?

"For I, the Lord, *do not change;* therefore you, O sons of Jacob, are not consumed" (Mal. 3:6 RSV).

Flying at night at 41,000 feet, we were "big, fat, dumb, and happy." My mind was flitting back and forth from flying the jet to the sales presentation I was scheduled to make the following day. The radio crackled shortly after we passed the Indianapolis VOR station—"Lear Jet N1001A, this is Indianapolis Center. You are five miles left of course!"

I did not like anyone correcting me and telling me to change when I knew I was right! I depressed my mike button and shot back, "My VOR needle is centered!" Indianapolis Center replied, "N1001A, have you checked your Omni Bearing Selector?"

Sure enough, having tracked High Altitude Jet Route J-110 inbound, and having crossed Indianapolis VOR, I had failed to put in the 085-degree outbound heading. I needed to alter my course just a few degrees before continuing on J-110 to New York.

In retrospect, this incident pointed out to me that just as in flying, we need to make proper changes in our personal flight path. At times we need to change our course in our spiritual walk in order to reach our God-directed goals.

First, the VOR signal is fixed and you cannot change it from within the aircraft. Most flight instructors drill into their students that they must not try to change the Omni Bearing Selector to match their course, but instead must *change their relationship* to the proper radio bearing or compass heading.

Second, we must not try to change the judgment of the Master Controller. I challenged the judgment call of the Indianapolis Center. It was I who needed to change course! "And she [Jerusalem] hath changed my judgements into wickedness more than the nations, and my statutes more than the countries that are round about her: for they have refused my ordinances and my statutes, they have not walked in them" (Ezek. 5:6). Let's dedicate ourselves to climbing on course! May God bless you and yours as we relax together, following the directions of our Master Controller.

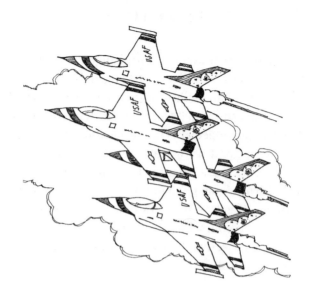

Is God Far Away?
He Has Not Moved!

15 Formation flying—fun or folly? It all depends on whether you had proper instruction. "He who teacheth himself formation flying—hath a fool for an instructor."

Trying to fly formation and following a veteran flight lead—that was fun! The tower was reluctant to clear us for takeoff as a "flight of two," but did after a few insistent pleas.

Preflight instructions, as I recall, included these:

1. "Don't be afraid to move in close." That reminded me of a Bible verse, "Can two walk together, except they be agreed?" (Amos 3:3 KJV).
2. "Tuck your wing tip in close behind and below my wing."
3. "Never take your eyes off of the N number on the side of my fuselage. Don't ever look at your flight or engine instruments."

This brief formation flight merely whetted my appetite for more, and I enjoyed doing it several times.

"My soul clings to you; your right hand upholds me" (Ps. 63:8). Just as formation flying has a boss, God, our Leader, is in charge of our spiritual missions. We should not take our eyes off of Him for even one second.

Due to an alleged malfunction, the 1982 Thunderbird leader could not pull up, and the diamond formation tragically bit the dust. The pilots were doing what they were trained to do—keep their eyes on their flight lead and follow him. Apparently the machine, not the man, had failed. Fortunately, the duty-bound, trained, Ambassadors in Blue continue on with their crowd-pleasing air shows.

As we embark on a new day, I hope and pray that all of us will keep our eyes on the Leader. He has never failed! "There failed [nothing] of any good thing which the Lord had spoken unto the house of Israel; all came to pass" (Josh. 21:45 KJV).

"No temptation [taking your eyes off of the Leader] has seized you except what is common to man. And God is faithful; he will not let you be tempted beyond what you can bear. But when you are tempted, he will also provide a way out so that you can stand up under it" (1 Cor. 10:13).

Is Prayer Needed on a Clear Day?

16 Silence—a single-engine bug-smasher (low-flying single-engine propeller airplane) quits, and you are carrying a passenger. Is it time to pray? Depends on several things, e.g., the surrounding terrain, altitude above the ground, glide ratio of the aircraft, distance from the nearest airport, and your faith and training as they relate to prayer. Turning 180 degrees to the nearest airport, I canceled my flight plan, stopped the windmilling propeller, and established a proper glide descent. My passenger asked, "Aren't you going to pray?" My reply was, "I prayed this morning and asked for God's protection, now it's time to fly." (I do, however, realize that prayer is a never-ending communication with God.) My newly designated "glider" made it to the airport. (Had to push it several yards to the pump—poor planning!)

Prayer—the mere use of the word causes division or peace, comfort or trouble, unity or conflict. Great early leaders of our country have prayed both in public and private. Presidents Washington and Lincoln, whose birthdays we commemorate each year, prayed to God for guidance and protection. The foundation they built on prayer has stood for many years. Some folks don't feel comfortable to pray out loud, and may even be offended if you ask them to do so. Aren't you glad we aren't all identical?

Starting the day off with prayer creates a pattern for me. I like to call it talking with God. I commune with God during the day as needs arise or other people are brought to mind. The Psalmist said: "As for me, I will call upon God, and the Lord shall save me. Evening, and morning, and at noon, will I pray, and cry aloud, and he shall hear my voice" (Ps. 55:16–17 KJV).

At what points during my journey through life should I pray? When I have a weak magneto and I'm on a night flight or on instruments—then I'll pray? When there are clear skies, flat terrain, and a near "zero time" engine twisting my propeller—why should I bother God with my prayers? How about praying when I just want to talk with God? "The Lord is near to all who call upon Him, to all who call upon Him in truth" (Ps. 145:18 RSV(?)).

Certainly the precision team, the United States Air Force Thunderbirds, does not need prayer prior to flight! Wrong! They are all well trained and experienced, and are backed up by a ground crew second to none. Capt. Jeff Rochelle, the left wing, told me that the crew gathers for prayer prior to *every* flight. Just as problems with the F-16 have to be dealt with based on the manual printed by General Dynamics, the manufacturer, so we need to pray to our Maker in order to keep our performance proper.

As complex decisions face both us and our beloved nation, let's not forget that our God wants us to talk with Him, and He wants to be involved in both our joys and our fears. Give Him a try!

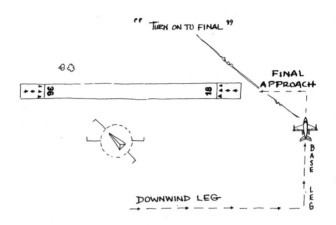

Don't Miss the Joy of "Voice Control"

17 Voice control! That term really acquired a new meaning at the Oklahoma City, Oklahoma, Tower Operator Training System in the Federal Aviation Administration Center. The TOTS system allows visual simulation of a tower control cab, with models for simulated pilots, motion, aircraft, and environmental conditions. Imagine being able to give voice commands to a simulated aircraft and have the aircraft respond precisely and immediately as your voice directs! Collisions do occur on this simulated system when students give improper commands.

"Ye shall walk [fly] after the Lord your God, and fear him, and keep his commandments, and obey his voice" (Deut. 13:4a). When I don't obey God's voice, there will likely be times when my life collides with someone else's life. The "screen collision" at TOTS does no damage to man or machine, but when "voices" other than God's interfere with my flight through life, disaster may result. Many a tower operator has rightfully lost patience with a pilot who failed to obey instructions and caused major disruptions in the flow of traffic. We know that God is patient, but at times He may allow us to get into trouble when His voice is ignored. He said, "If you listen carefully to the voice of the LORD your God and do what is right in his eyes, if you pay attention to his commands and keep all his decrees, I will not bring on you any of the diseases I brought on the Egyptians, for I am the LORD, who heals you" (Exod. 15:26). God specializes in crash avoidance, but He also has a great realignment shop. I know—I've been there.

The simulated airfield layout has two parallel runways and one cross runway, as well as varied aircraft arrival and departure patterns and landing options. It can depict day or night, wet runways, and clear sky or limited visibility caused by fog or low ceilings. Voice recognition and response capability allows instructors to vary the program. They can monitor training at all control tower positions and insert changes to a scenario. These include adding or deleting aircraft in the scenario, or introducing equipment malfunctions. If they wish to simulate an emergency situation, instructors can also act as pseudo-pilots.

During rush times or emergencies, many of us have spoken in haste and given incomplete or erroneous information. The Psalmist had a similar problem: "In my alarm I said, 'I am cut off from your sight!' Yet you heard my cry for mercy when I called to you for help" (Ps. 31:22). Both pilots and tower operators can miss communication, but the Psalmist *knew* that God was always listening. His answers may be delayed, but never forgotten!

Logicon, along with the Federal Aviation Administration, has developed the TOTS system. It allows for an aircraft to be seen and controlled from a location seven miles from the airport, and it covers the entire airport and the tower control cab itself. The result is superior training combined with surprising economy.

The United States Air Force and Civil Air Patrol have taught thousands of cadets and senior members the importance of obedience to command—but it is up to us individually to be responsive to God's voice in our lives. Are you tuned in for the next "voice command?"

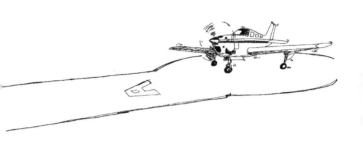

Is This Bucket of Bolts
Fit to Fly?

18 Doing the preflight can be a real pain. You're in a hurry to go, passengers are fretting, and depending on how sophisticated your aircraft is, it can take a long time to go through each item. The preflight test and the engine run-up test(s) are not only a good idea, they're required in the FAA Regulation. Failure to conduct them may prove to "ruin your whole day."

Israel, under stress from Pharaoh, was repeatedly denied entrance into the wilderness to worship. God actually was preparing and planning their escape and return to the promised land. Testing Pharaoh with plagues must have resulted in a growing faith in the lives of the Israelites. Then came the ultimate test: "On that same night I will pass through Egypt and strike down every firstborn—both men and animals—and I will bring judgment on all the gods of Egypt. I am the LORD. The blood will be a sign for you on the houses where you are; and when I see the blood [of the slain sacrificial animal, according to God's checklist], I will pass over you. No destructive plague will touch you when I strike Egypt" (Exod. 12:12–13). All who used God's checklist were spared death! God was both testing and directing the lives of Jacob's descendants—testing Israel, like an aircraft run-up, to see whether they were fit for the trip.

The disciples, in their relationship to Christ, the Master Instructor, were also tested. "I will smite the shepherd, and the sheep of the flock shall be scattered abroad" (Matt. 26:31b). And scatter they did! They failed the run-up test! Later the Spirit of God moved and they united as a force "fit to fly." They were given another chance. We are fortunate that both God and man have given us many "second chances" to redeem ourselves after a checkout failure!

Testing the equipment, controls, RPM, and EGT (exhaust gas temperature) seems mundane on a familiar aircraft, but use of the preflight test must become an ingrained habit. Forgetting one item in a checklist, or not using the manual at all, calls for a pink slip on a check-ride. After a friend of mine, who was known not to use the preflight test, failed to survive a routine jet takeoff, I always had students go back to the first item in the preflight manual if they passed over any single item in the long list of pages of checks prior to takeoff. That didn't make for the greatest of interpersonal cockpit relationships at the moment—but it did create great preflight habits in both new pilots and those who transitioned into our new jet.

God has His own checklist for us—it is the Holy Bible! "Vindicate me, O LORD, for I have walked in my integrity, I have also trusted in the Lord; I shall not slip. Examine me, O Lord, and prove me; try my mind and my heart" (Ps. 26:1–2). The established Operations Manual (God's written Word) and the aircraft manufacturer's operations manual can keep us out of a lot of trouble—they are truly designed as life savers!

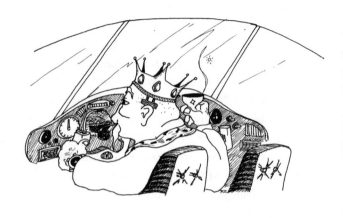

Dictator
or Consensus Maker?

19 An acrid smell filled the cockpit as sparks shot out from under the panel in what appeared to be an electrical short! Midnight darkness, three frightened staff members in my aircraft—that was a nervous cockpit environment! What to do?

Decisions that I make when my actions—be they right or wrong—involve others should be weighed more carefully than those that affect only me. Dictatorial cockpit rule is not always the soundest of approaches. Fortunately, cockpit management has taken on a different approach in recent years. Moses, leading Israel out of Egypt, was given some management principles by his father-in-law, Jethro: "'What is this you are doing for the people? Why do you alone sit as judge, while all these people stand around you from morning till evening?' . . . Moses' father-in-law replied, 'What you are doing is not good. . . . The work is too heavy for you; you cannot handle it alone. Listen now to me and I will give you some advice, and may God be with you. . . . Teach them the decrees and laws, and show them the way to live and the duties they are to perform. But select capable men from all the people, men who fear God, trustworthy men who hate dishonest gain, and appoint them as officials over thousands, hundreds, fifties, and tens. . . . That will make your load lighter, because they will share it with you'" (Exod. 18:14–22). Shared responsibilities work.

The one-man committee does not work in the long run. Both God's Word and experience show us that we need to "bounce it off" someone else prior to taking action. I try to let someone read my letters, memos, agendas, etc., prior to implementation. As I look back, I'm sure that procedure has saved me many a heartburn. "Where no counsel is, the people fall: but in the multitude of counselors there is safety" (Prov. 11:14).

Emergency procedures were followed in my aircraft that night:

1. Electrical master switch off.
2. Pull all circuit breakers.
3. Isolate the problem. If isolation is possible, turn on the working circuits.
4. Land as soon as practicable.

Items 1 and 2 were easy; however, I could not isolate the problem. Time for an airborne committee meeting! There was no full-service field nearby—a landing at a small airport with no service wouldn't solve the problem. While continuing on, I gave the three staff members the options: (a) land at the closest small airstrip and sleep (who knows where, maybe under the wings); or (b) continue on to my own base, where there was a nicely lighted runway, with no control tower for a simpler approach, plus good mechanics and our own beds.

Asking all of them to take extra observations for other aircraft, and using well-lighted highways for navigation, we agreed to press on. Using my flashlight allowed me to remain at the proper flight altitude and also observe engine instruments and the whiskey compass, i.e., a compass with non-freezing alcohol. We reached home base without incident. My staff was all in favor of my actions—we were a cohesive group. Allowing questions and input made it a happier, more united trip. No, we were no safer acting as a unit—I could have arbitrarily said, "We are going on."—But asking for input from my passengers made us a working group that was willing to bear the consequences.

May God help us to be leaders—not just dictators.

Unfamiliar Routes—
Can You Handle It?

20 Change! Change! Why do I have to live in a world of constant change? The Bible predicts that knowledge will increase— the result of more knowledge is change.

"But thou, O Daniel, shut up the words, and seal the book, even to the time of the end: many shall run to and fro, and knowledge shall be increased" (Dan. 12:4). Are we ever living in a time when knowledge is increasing!

Global Positioning System testing and applications have just begun in aviation in recent years. GPS is already being used by the military, car rental agencies, and search and rescue operations. When completed, GPS will be unbelievably more accurate and easier to fly than the old (within my lifetime) *A* and *N* signal. But it will require change in both aircraft and ground equipment. Being surrounded with change can be very frustrating and expensive. "Teach me your way, O LORD; lead me in a straight path because of my oppressors" (Ps. 27:11). What man is doing today in aviation and other fields is what God has been trying to do for centuries with man—namely, have us follow a straight path.

Terminal control areas and control zones have gone through some big changes recently. To keep abreast of these changes requires constant vigilance and training. My frame of reference in local operation had to change when I came to Tucson International Airport—my recent flying had been in central Oregon's non-control-tower-operated airports. Having been away from Tucson for several years, I was almost ready to ask for progressive taxi instructions (ground control then directs you each step of the way as you switch from one taxiway to another) when directed to taxi past airliners, F-16s, and a myriad of taxiway identifiers. Change is constant, but most of the rules of flight do not change!

So what can I do about change? Professional counselors suggest that each of us needs a firm foundation or an anchor to hold on to during troubled times. "Because God wanted to make the unchanging nature of his purpose very clear to the heirs of what was promised, he confirmed it with an oath. God did this so that, by two unchangeable things in which it is impossible for God to lie, we who have fled to take hold of the hope offered to us may be greatly encouraged. We have this hope as an *anchor* for the soul, firm and secure. It enters the inner sanctuary behind the curtain, where Jesus, who went before us, has entered on our behalf. He has become a high priest forever, in the order of Melchizedek" (Heb. 6:17–20).

What about trying a tested and sure way? "For I am the Lord, I change not" (Mal. 3:6a). Whether it's a job change, vocational change, or a geographic change—put your trust in God! He never changes.

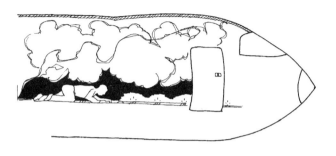

Get on Your Knees and Follow the Light

21 The airline passenger seat was comfortable. The cabin attendant had us all seated and ready for takeoff. A few minutes later, the cabin filled with smoke, and at my eye level I could see virtually nothing. The emergency exit lights came on. "Get down and follow the track lighting on the floor. The little lights will be red at the exits," said the cabin attendant.

This scene took place, not at flight level 410 (nearly 8 miles high), but at the Federal Aviation

Administration Training Center in Oklahoma City, Oklahoma. The cabin was a section of an airliner; the smoke was simulated. The FAA, along with NASA and the airline industry, designed the lighting system for passenger airlines in case of crashes and the resulting fire and smoke. Emergency situations in both airplanes and buildings usually demand getting down into breathable air and following a known path to safety. The Psalmist also asked us to "kneel before the LORD our Maker" (Ps. 95:6).

When the Israelites were doing things their way—not unlike the song "I Did It My Way"—God asked Moses to come up the mountain and receive the Ten Commandments. Moses "bow[ed] his head toward the earth, and worshiped" (Exod. 34:8 RSV), and then took the tables of the law down to the people.

If we as a nation and as individuals want to survive national "cabin fire and smoke," isn't it time to fall on our knees now and follow the light? "If my people, which are called by my name, shall humble themselves, and pray, and seek my face, and turn from their wicked ways; then will I hear from heaven, and will forgive their sin, and will heal their land" (2 Chron. 7:14 KJV). My prayer is "God heal our land and begin with me."

Paul, writing to the Church at Ephesus, says:

> In Him and through faith in him we may approach God with freedom and confidence. I ask you, therefore, not to be discouraged because

of my sufferings for you, which are your glory. For this reason *I kneel* before the Father, from whom his whole family in heaven and on earth derives its name. I pray that out of his glorious riches he may strengthen you with power through his Spirit in your inner being, so that Christ may dwell in your hearts through faith. And I pray that you, being rooted and established in love, may have power, together with all the saints, to grasp how wide and long and high and deep is the love of Christ, and to know this love that surpasses knowledge, that you may be filled to the measure of all the fullness of God. Now to him who is able to do immeasurably more than all we ask or imagine, according to his power that is at work within us, to him be glory in the church and in Christ Jesus throughout all generations, for ever and ever! Amen. (Eph. 3:12, italics mine)

"FLY RIGHT! — 200 PLUS PEOPLE IN THIS PLANE DEPEND ON YOU!"

Can One Person Make a Difference?

22 Can I make a difference? Do my vote, my actions, and my taking a stand and keeping a vision alive for America make a difference in the place where it all happens—the national and world center of power—our nation's capital? As I looked down from my flight out of Washington National Airport, my heart cried out to God in prayer for our nation. Debts going out of sight with no apparent stopping—morals hitting bottom with no nationwide attempt to put on the brakes! No cognizant evidence of the dire situation in which we find ourselves. No one pulling the chute release handle, as on a test plane, to stop our flat spin to destruction.

Again—can I make a difference?

First of all, we may hide behind the numbers: "What can I do among 248,709,873 Americans (U.S. census figure, 1990) to make any kind of impact?" Kind of like a gnat trying to lift a spacecraft into orbit. Wrong! History, both Biblical and secular, gives us countless instances where one person made the difference. I personally can make a difference, and by the grace of Almighty God, I will. I pledge to God not to give up!

Noah, following God's command, made a difference—as did Abraham, David, Peter, Paul, and others.

- 1645: One vote gave Oliver Cromwell control of England.
- 1649: One vote caused King Charles I of England to be executed.
- 1800: One vote kept Aaron Burr, later charged with treason, from becoming President.
- 1845: One vote difference brought Texas into the Union. A single vote also brought in California, Oregon, and Washington.
- 1868: One vote saved Andrew Johnson from impeachment.

- 1876: One vote elected Rutherford B. Hayes to the Presidency. The man in the electoral college who cast that vote was an Indiana representative who was also elected by one vote.
- 1923: By one vote, Adolf Hitler became the Nazi party leader.
- John F. Kennedy's margin of victory over Nixon was only one vote per precinct.
- Florence Nightingale, whose own family opposed her career in the field of nursing, made a big difference.

Many of you are out there standing for God and for what's right. Let's all join the movement to return our nation to spiritual and fiscal responsibility. God is still looking for men and women to "stand in the gap" for Him: "And I [God] sought for a man among them, that should make up the hedge, and stand in the gap before me for the land, that I should not destroy it; but I found none" (Ezek. 22:30). More and more people are speaking out for God in the military, sports, schools, and colleges. People in the field of medicine are learning that our spiritual health has a lot to do with our physical well-being. As we maintain our inner spiritual strength, we will also be able to fight evil. Recently one of our major television networks is said to have lost $3 million due to boycotts of the products that sponsored violence and filth. One man spearheaded this movement. A change is in the wind. Let's become a part of it. Our talented young people are worth fighting for! What if no one listens to you? God told Ezekiel that if they didn't listen, they would at least know that God's servant had been among them. May our God direct and bless you in your important area of personal responsibility.

Life Is Real—
Death Is Certain

23 *Oh, no! I'm going to crash!* My F-16 fighter is inverted; up seems to be down; down seems to be up; the heads-up display doesn't make sense; external forces are in control! Impact with mother earth is not far away. *Harms, get yourself back to the basics,* I told myself. I got my mind and eyes back on the old familiar "eight ball." *Now get yourself right side up.* As I did, everything started to fall back in place. My flight was in an F-16 fighter flight simulator at the Arizona Air National Guard in Tucson, Arizona, and I had really never left the ground. I'm sure that Mr. Dave Castillo, at the simulator control panel, had a few laughs! Thanks to Lt. Col. Ron Shoopman and Major Mark Besich for arranging my simulator time. Did you know that the Armed Forces are training more and more young pilots for the defense of our country? (Why don't you check it out, and consider joining an elite branch of the Armed Forces.)

As I thought about simulators versus actual flying, my mind shifted to the reality of life and its complexities. Television violence; deadly computer-generated kids' games; and the media hype of shootings, stabbings, and beatings have put us into a scenario where many of our youth have no regard for life, death, or the consequences of improper behavior patterns. External pressures are molding us into the unknown and unwanted. Friends—we are not in a flight-through-life simulator! Life is real! "Therefore this is what I will do to you, Israel, and because I will do this to you, prepare to meet your God, O Israel" (Amos 4:12). Those words are as appropriate for us today as they were for Israel. Let's not rush through our journey in life as if there were no tomorrow. As I had to do in the simulator, let's pause and reflect on God's basic laws and desires for us, His creation.

When Hezekiah was sick, the Bible says that the prophet Isaiah came to him and said, "This is what the LORD says: Put your house in order, because you are going to die; you will not recover" (2 Kings 20:1b). Hezekiah was not flying in a simulator, where the wrong moves damage only your pride. He was, as we are, facing reality. History shows us that Hezekiah prayed and God spared his life. Hezekiah set his life in order, and God gave him another fifteen years of life.

Several times, as I overcorrected, I said, "I'm sorry" to Dave, the simulator operator. My initial F-16 approach pattern was abysmal. At the point where I knew I'd crash if I continued on my landing approach, I gave full power with afterburner on and "blew out of there." Dave gave me another chance. "You are forgiving and good, O Lord, abounding in love to all who call to you. Hear my prayer, O Lord; listen to my cry for mercy" (Ps. 86:5–6). "If we confess our sins, he is faithful and just and will forgive us our sins and purify us from all unrighteousness" (1 John 1:9). Feel like you need help? Give Him a call!

Does Your Baggage
Baffle You?

24 Baggage—We wait at the carousel; we check the weight of our two-plus pieces of luggage. Are the bag tags, with our current address, securely attached? Some travelers take ocean cruises just so they won't have to handle the endless baggage problems!

Memory reminds me of a flight from New York City to upstate New York to pick up the wife of a famous movie star. Not only was she very late, but her baggage would have filled a farm-size pickup truck. As we waited for her arrival, an ice storm of some magnitude drew near, and we became nervous about getting out of this isolated airstrip with no weather reporting or navigational aids. Our timing of the seconds between the sighting of the lightning and the thunder peal told us the storm was not far away. Since we were not flying a C-5 transport but a small business jet, deciding which baggage to take consumed another thirty minutes. We barely got airborne before the storm hit.

As you have just started another new day, may I suggest that you leave yesterday's "old baggage" behind? The hurts you have experienced, disappointments (they may truly be God's appointments), frustrations, and lost opportunities—why not let go? We have had joys and disappointments, victories and losses, aspirations that worked and those that turned sour—but God's family has a tremendous past, present, and future! So, as the Bible says, "forgetting those things which are behind, and reaching forth unto those things which are before, I press toward the mark for the prize" (Philippians 3:13b–14a). Moses led the children of Israel to the promised land; their failures came when they looked back at "old baggage." They argued with God's chosen leaders and said to Moses and Aaron: "If only we had died by the LORD's hand in Egypt! There we sat around pots of meat and ate all the food we wanted, but you have brought us out into this desert to starve this entire assembly to death" (Exod. 16:3). Little did they know that the "baggage" they were carrying would keep them from the blessing of the promised land.

Our baggage problem in upstate New York caused me to be in a forty-five-minute holding pattern over LaGuardia Airport in icing conditions. No fun, since at that early stage in development, we did not have the automatic recycling of the heat blanket in the engine nacelle de-ice system. (Incidentally, our personal baggage problems may "ice out" some worthy fellow traveler.)

As our founding father, George Washington, prayed before the battle of his life, let us pray for our nation's leaders and for ourselves that our renewed vision will take all of us ever onward and upward! (Minus old baggage, of course.)

Thank God, I'm Still Alive

25 "You're dead, Mr. Harms—the jet you were flying crashed!" said the second shift supervisor, as he turned white as a sheet at the Lear Jet factory entrance. Being thankful that I was very much alive, I started asking questions about the jet that I was to have flown—which now was no more. Was I really thankful? And how would I show it, in coming days, to God and others?

Thankful—what a powerful word! But what does it really mean to be thankful? Webster says thankful is "to show or express appreciation or gratitude." Because of God's protecting hand over me and my having missed piloting that fateful flight—would I now really show and express thanksgiving?

"Sacrifice thank offerings to God, fulfill your vows to the Most High, and call upon me in the day of trouble; I will deliver you, and you will honor me" (Ps. 50:14). How often have we given thanks to God and paid any of our vows? What became of promises we made to help a needy person, a homeless child, a person who has lost a job or loved one? We need not look across the expanse of the ocean; we have those who have problems that we can help solve in our very own neighborhoods.

Would it be proper if I changed the word *thanksgiving* to *thanksliving?* Doing that would result in a 365-day-a-year adventure. The lives of all around us would certainly sense the difference.

The jet that crashed left no survivors. I was still on the crew flight plan. Just ten minutes prior to departure, an unannounced Lear Jet prospect came into my office, and since I was the only marketing person left at the factory, I replaced myself on the flight. I took the chief pilot of the prospective client out for an early dinner, and returned to the factory later that night to hear the sad news. God had seen fit to spare my life! During the first several months after this incident, I was keenly aware of the value I must place on my spared life. What was I going to do to show God and others my thankfulness for being alive? I trust I have been at least partially responsive in showing thanksgiving to God and others for His goodness to me.

Many of you have had numerous close calls. Some of you have shared them with me. Are we using these "extra bonus days" to the glory of God by living a life of thanksgiving?

Has our national Thanksgiving Day ever caused us to sacrifice? Have we shared our faith with others by sacrificing time and talents to a lonely or sad person during our celebration of Thanksgiving Day and all the rest of the year? In 1863, President Abraham Lincoln declared the last Thursday in November "a day of thanksgiving and praise to our beneficent Father"! "And let them sacrifice the sacrifice of thanksgiving, and declare his works with rejoicing" (Ps. 107:22 KJV).

Not one of us is on earth without a purpose. Are we thankful for *life*, health, friends and our freedom? Have you thanked a friend recently just for being there for you?

Don't Be Afraid to Turn Back—the Life You Save May Be Your Own

26 Snow was swirling, visibility deteriorating, my passengers were anxious—and I was in command and responsible! The flight to celebrate Christmas in Iowa had been without incident. For the return trip, the weather briefer—from a distant weather station—had encouraged me to take the Visual Flight Rules flight in my plane, which had no de-icing equipment. Should I jeopardize five lives and "try to make it home"? *No*—here is where we do a 180 (turn back to where we came from).

My passengers pressured me into continuing by saying, "Look what disruptions you'll cause both for school and work if we don't get back." My response by this time did not take much deliberation: "Five funerals would disrupt things a lot more!"

Sometimes God tells an entire nation to make a 180-degree turn. "If my people, who are called by my name, will humble themselves and pray and seek my face and *turn* from their wicked ways, then will I hear from heaven and will forgive their sin and will heal their land" (2 Chron. 7:14 emphasis added). As we face the many weighty decisions that life brings on us with our families and friends, let us be assured that He will guide us through our difficult decisions. "You guide me with your counsel, and afterward you will take me into glory" (Ps. 73:24).

Two days after my 180-degree turn and flight cancellation, we flew home—and our path of flight took us over the hills on the Missouri River where a plane full of people had crashed during the same storm we had waited out. There were no more arguments in the plane about whether a proper decision had been made a few days back. When circumstances prevent you from accomplishing your desired schedule or path—wait on the Lord! "Repent, then, and turn to God, so that your sins may be wiped out, that times of refreshing may come from the Lord" (Acts 3:19). The word *repent* means "to turn back." After all, He is in command and His guidance will be for our good.

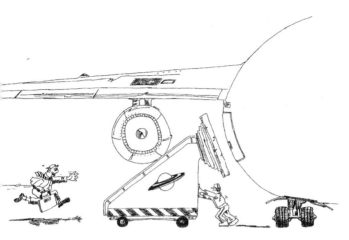

Stop the Push-Back: My ~~Friend Didn't~~ Make Gate in Time!

27 My airline flight was canceled due to a mechanical problem—and I was frantic! The place for my meeting was Atlanta, not my home base at Wichita, Kansas. What should I do? God bless the strangers in our lives who so often assist by giving much-needed advice. This complete stranger told me that airline XYZ had a flight to Atlanta, and that they were accepting tickets from my "down" airline. I rushed and got my ticket validated and confirmed. In just a few brief minutes I was sitting in my assigned seat and poring through my briefcase. As the captain announced our departure, I looked up, and two things caught my attention. Number 1 was that the portable steps were being pushed back. Number 2 was that the stranger who had helped me get onto my flight was running for the steps. For a reason unknown to me, he had been delayed. The stewardess refused to stop the action and load the passenger. I rushed to the cockpit and told the captain about the situation. He then ordered the door opened and allowed the passenger on board.

I've thought of this experience many times when I deal with friends who have not as yet made their peace with God. But when I think of the command of Christ to go into all the world and give the good news, then I stop and again try to assume my responsibility. Jesus gave us the parable of the man who prepared a banquet. When there was still room, the following happened: "'Sir,' the servant said, 'what you ordered has been done, but there is still room.' Then the master told his servant, 'Go out to the roads and country lanes and *make* them come in, so that my house will be full'" (Luke 14:22–23). I am the first to know from personal experience that you may risk a friendship by sharing God's plan of salvation with a friend. Maybe you can begin by sharing your personal experience as to how you received the peace of God and the forgiveness of sin.

When I asked the captain of the airliner to take aboard my new-found friend, he stopped all action and did so. I find no hint in the Bible that at Christ's coming, when the Lord returns to earth for deceased Christians and those of us who will still be alive, there will be time to ask the Captain to take on another passenger. "So, as the Holy Spirit says: 'Today, if you hear his voice do not harden your hearts as you did in the rebellion, during the time of testing in the desert'" (Heb. 3:7–8).

Friend, if you have never helped someone turn his or her life over to Christ, use the pages in the back of this book (Plan of Salvation) and help a friend prepare to board the final flight.

"For the Lord himself will come down from heaven, with a loud command, with the voice of the archangel and with the trumpet call of God, and the dead in Christ will rise first. After that, we who are still alive and are left will be caught up together with them in the clouds to meet the Lord in the air. And so we will be with the Lord forever." (1 Thess. 4:16–17)

See you on the last flight!

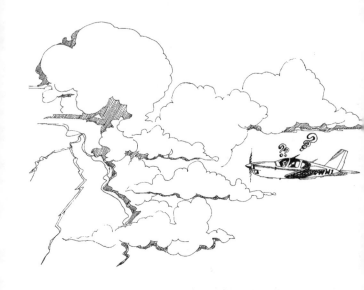

Lost in the Clouds – What Do I Do Now?

28 As a child, one of the hardest things for me to do was to admit to my mother that I had done a wrong, e.g., taken the missing cookies, spilled the flour, left the henhouse open, etc. It hasn't changed much in later years. I still do not like to admit a wrong, but I have had very little trouble admitting I'm in trouble when I fly. A temporary mistake that is not corrected can lead to a permanent unhealthy solution.

Air traffic controllers have been able for years to direct—give vectors to—pilots who are lost, but the first step is for the pilot to realize and admit he is in trouble. Some rules to follow if in trouble:

1. *Climb* to a higher altitude. If you're in a mountainous area, this will minimize the chances of planting your aircraft into a "granite cloud." In a spiritual sense we also need to climb. Jesus went up into a mountain to pray. Have you had any "mountain-top" experiences lately? "After he had dismissed them, he went up on a mountainside by himself to pray. When evening came, he was there alone" (Matt. 14:23).

2. *Confess* to the controller what type of problem you have run into. Tell him everything! I have had friends who failed to give all the details of their problem to the controller and perished. It is far easier to explain on paper what you did wrong *after* you are on the ground than to have your surviving family explain what might have been the nature of your wrong flying habits. In your relationship to God, your sins—of either omission or commission—need to be cleared up. "If we confess our sins, he is faithful and just and will forgive us our sins and purify us from

all unrighteousness. If we claim we have not sinned, we make him out to be a liar and his word has no place in our lives" (1 John 1:9).

3. *Comply* with the instructions of the controller, who is in a dry and warm cubicle and can think more clearly than you, you who are being kicked around in your aircraft by unfriendly air currents. As you have embarked on your spiritual mission through life, listen to the Word of God and the Holy Spirit's inner voice as He prompts you to take whatever action is needed. "If you obey my commands, you will remain in my love, just as I have obeyed my Father's commands and remain in his love. I have told you this so that my joy may be in you and that your joy may be complete" (John 15:10–11).

4. *Communicate* with whoever is giving you the directions. Sometimes the message will be relayed via a friendly airliner or military jet overhead, since you may be in a low area with mountains interfering. Did it ever seem to you that your prayers were hitting the ceiling and bouncing back? Maybe there is a reason for unanswered prayers. As a pilot examines his position periodically during the entire flight, he must check out where he is in his travels. "When you ask, you do not receive, because you ask with wrong motives, that you may spend what you on your pleasures."

(James 4:3 [See also Isa. 59:2, Ps. 66:18]. Keep on communicating! God does hear your every word. He may also communicate through others and thus get the message to you. "Then the man and his wife heard the sound of the LORD God as he was walking in the garden in the cool of the day, and they hid from the LORD God among the trees of the garden" (Gen. 3:8). This verse clearly indicates that God's plan for us is to communicate with Him. It's *not* a long-distance call!

Just "Mike Fright" May Cause an Accident!

29 Having taken my primary instruction on a grass landing strip, my solo flight left me talking only to myself and God. No radio or tower. Maybe the single-engine bug smasher would not have been able to get off the ground with the added weight of a generator and radio system. Wichita, Kansas, was the closest control tower, and there was no other communication with any other control agency. What a rude awakening when I first had to fly into a controlled airport. Was I ever scared! I had a real dose of "mike fright." You can get so involved with wanting to say the right things in the right manner and sequence that you can forget to fly the airplane. In hindsight, my instructor might have had me listen to a few recordings of tower talk.

Has the organized Christian church used such lofty terms and tones that the average seeker, searching for the truth of God's communication with man, thinks he has to use certain "Biblical phraseology" in order to be heard by God? Have Christians—those of us who claim to know God through Christ in a personal way—made the appearance of being "holy Joes" to the extent that the earnest seeker has been turned off? Thank God that there is a movement in public prayer of speaking in everyday common language.

If you really would like to get over your "mike fright" (fear of talking to God) and come to God through Christ—just say what's on your heart. Follow the steps that are listed in the back of this book (Plan of Salvation). If you do, you will never have to fear talking to Him again. Incidentally, I am talking about private communion with God, not praying in public. Public prayer may take years of private study and prayer prior to feeling comfortable doing it. Friend, even *before* you get into some really serious problem, open your mind and heart to Him. "In the same way, the Spirit helps us in our weakness. We do not know what we ought to pray for, but the Spirit himself intercedes for us with groans that words cannot express. And he who searches our hearts knows the mind of the Spirit, because the Spirit intercedes for the saints in accordance with God's will" (Romans 8:26–27). He's listening!

He's tuned in!

It's Not What You Know, but Whom You Know

30 You need to see the president of the United States. You buy a ticket to Washington National Airport, rent a cab, and away you go. Best suit, shiny shoes, power tie, and a new haircut! But to your chagrin, the guards don't let you even close to the president.

You stretch to your full height and demand to see the president. Then you blurt out: "Listen, I arranged for private jets to fly him around on his campaign; I have to see him. Look at all of the good I've done for him. Now move over and let me in. I've voted for him in the past. I've prayed for him; I support his programs and handed out his party's literature. I've done it all." I would be rudely pushed to the side. (Incidentally, I did all of the above for Richard Nixon, and I'm sure that if I had tried, I still wouldn't have gotten in to see him without an appointment.)

Just about this time you see the president's son come down the hall. You greet him, since you know him, and without any hindrance you walk past the guards and into the president's private office. How did you do that? You knew the president's son. It's that simple. "For it is by grace you have been saved, through faith—and this not from yourselves, it is the gift of God—*not by works,* so that no one can boast" (Eph. 2:8–9).

Fellow traveler, you won't see the Father without knowing the Son. Period! End of sentence! *But*—you say—*I belong to church. I do visitations for the church. You should see the donations I rack up over a year. Check my IRS tax form.* Want to walk into heaven's gate? You have to know the Son. "'Do not let your hearts be troubled. Trust in God; trust also in me. In my Father's house are many rooms; if it were not so, I would have told you. I am going there to prepare a place for you. And if I go and prepare a place for you, I will come back and take you to be with me that you also may be where I am. You know the way to the place where I am going.' Thomas said to him, 'Lord, we don't know where you are going, so how can we know the way?' Jesus answered, 'I am the way and the truth and the life. No one comes to the Father except through me. If you really knew me, you would know my Father as well. From now on, you do know him and have seen him'" (John 14:1–7).

Back to the Barn

31 I'm sure the crew on the jet didn't think the day would be anything but routine: Climb to and maintain flight level 410 (41,000 feet). Easy enough, and at that time very few jets flew up there except military. Little traffic, and the biggest concern would be that boredom would lull the crew to sleep. All went well on the climb out. The CJ610 engines were pushing the jet like a rocket. Level at flight level 410, reduce engine RPM to 93 percent, punch the autopilot, and relax with your soda. En route frequency changes,

Omni Bearing Selector changes—all was routine until time to begin the descent. Ease the thrust levers back and begin the gradual descent. "Who fastened the knurl knob so tightly?" Checking it, they found that it was loose. A stark realization: The thrust levers were stuck! Since this was an emergency, the crew reported it to Air Traffic Control.

Without being able to reduce power, bringing the jet down would cause it to fly so fast that it would break the sound barrier and destroy the aircraft. Engineers believed that the tip tanks would come off first and then the tail. How would they get down to land? After communicating with the factory at Wichita, and determining there was enough fuel on board to reach Wichita, the jet headed for our city. Why Wichita? Number 1, McConnell Air Force Base has one of the longest runways around; five miles long, I recall. Number 2, Wichita was the *home of the malfunctioning jet*. Get the airplane "back to the barn" so we could analyze the problem.

The jet headed for McConnell, and when it was time to descend, the pilots shut down one of the emergency fuel shutoff switches. When arriving in the traffic pattern, they shut off the other one and landed on the long runway, dead stick (no power).

So—the jet was created in Wichita, and now it had returned to its creator. "So God created man in his own image, in the image of God he created him; male and female he created them" (Gen. 1:27). Don't try to solve your problems without the help of your

Creator. Friend, take the wings of prayer and go back to the barn. You're cleared for the approach. "I have swept away your offenses like a cloud, your sins like the morning mist. Return to me, for I have redeemed you" (Isa. 44:22).

The fix: Condensation from inside the fuselage had frozen the cables in place in the belly of the aircraft. A few weep holes solved the problem.

(Oh yes, even after this experience, the pilots were not given a glider rating.)

Plan of Salvation

Eternal Life Is Based on God's Love

> For God so loved the world, that He gave His only begotten Son, that whoever believes in him should not perish, but have eternal life. (John 3:16 KJV)

Abundant Life

> I came that they might have life, and have it abundantly. (John 10:10b RSV)

Obviously most people are not experiencing the abundant life that Christ promised, nor are they assured of their eternal destiny. Fact number two explains why.

2. Man's Problem Is Sin, Which Separates Him from God

According to the Bible, sin is:

- Missing the mark—a falling short of God's standard of perfect holiness
- A condition within man that results in separation from God

Sin is revealed by attitudes as well as actions.

Man Is Sinful

> For all have sinned and fall short of the glory of God. (Rom. 3:23)

> For whoever keeps the whole law and yet stumbles in one point, he has become guilty of all. (James 2:10)

According to the above definition and verses, do you think that you have sinned? Do you know the penalty of sin? Let me explain.

The Penalty of Sin

"For the wages [penalty] of sin is death" (Rom. 6:23a). This is not merely physical death, but

GOOD LIFE CHURCH EDUCATION MONEY BAPTISM

MAN
(SINFUL)

spiritual death, which results in eternal separation from God.

Because of man's sin, there is a great gap that separates man from God. He has tried to bridge this gap through many means—a good life, church work, education, money, baptism, etc. But God demands a payment so high for the penalty of sin that all of man's efforts still fall short of God's glory.

Since God is holy and just, He must judge man's sin.

> And inasmuch as it is appointed for men to die once and after this comes judgment . . . (Heb. 9:27 NAS)

The third fact gives us the only remedy to death, eternal separation, and judgment.

3. GOD'S PROVISION IS JESUS CHRIST ALONE

His Death Paid the Penalty for Sin

> But God demonstrates His own love toward us, in that while we were yet sinners, Christ died for us. (Rom. 5:8 NAS)

> Knowing that you were not redeemed with perishable things . . . , but with precious blood, as of a lamb unblemished and spotless, the blood of Christ. (1 Pet. 1:18–19)

105

His Resurrection Defeated Death

> Christ died for our sins. . . . He was buried. . . .
> He was raised on the third day according to the
> Scriptures. . . . He appeared to Cephas, then to
> the twelve. After that He appeared to more than
> five hundred. . . . (1 Cor. 15:3–6)

Christ Is the Only Way Acceptable to God

> For there is one God, and one mediator also be-
> tween God and men, the man
> Christ Jesus. (1 Tim. 2:5 NAS)

> Jesus said to him, I am
> the way, and the truth,
> and the life; no one
> comes to the Father, but
> through Me. (John 14:6
> NAS)

Since man always falls short
of satisfying God's just de-
mands, He sent Christ, who was the sinless God-
Man, to pay the penalty of death
on the cross for us. He alone
bridged this gap. No other sub-
stitute is acceptable to God.
God demands a perfect sacrifice, and this is why He had to
take the initiative to find a suit-
able remedy.

Though Christ died for all men, obviously all are not Christians. It is not enough to just know these three facts. Each one of us has just one responsibility.

4. MAN'S DECISION REQUIRES FAITH IN JESUS CHRIST

We Must Believe in Christ

> But as many as received Him, to them He gave the right to become children of God, even to those who believe in His name. (John 1:12 NAS)

> He who hears My word, and believes Him who sent Me has eternal life, and does not come into judgment, but has passed out of death into life. (John 5:24 NAS)

Eternal Life Is Through Faith Alone

> For by grace you have been saved, through faith; and that not of yourselves, it is the gift of God; not as a result of works, that no one should boast. (Eph. 2:8–9)

This diagram represents two kinds of lives. Which side best represents your life at this time? Which side would you like to have represent your life?

MAN

A LIFE WHICH HAS
SIN
FRUSTRATION
LACK OF PURPOSE
UNSURE OF ETERNAL
DESTINY

A LIFE WHICH HAS
FORGIVENESS
PEACE
ABUNDANT LIFE
ETERNAL LIFE

What are you believing in (trusting on) right now to get you to heaven and enable you to have the Life on the right side?

Check the space(s) that apply to your belief.

- ☐ Living a good life
- ☐ Baptism
- ☐ Believing God exists
- ☐ Following the Ten Commandments
- ☐ Believing what Christ did for me is sufficient alone
- ☐ Other

What does the Bible say is the correct answer?

To believe in Christ (to receive Him) means to put one's complete trust in Jesus Christ alone, to forgive all of his sins, and give him eternal life. It is not Christ plus something—a good life, baptism, etc. It is receiving a free gift of God's grace by faith alone based only on the benefits of Christ's death, burial, and resurrection.

Would you like to take this step by faith in Christ *alone* and be assured of the promise that Christ offers? The following explains how.

Here is a suggested prayer, which you may want to use to express your decision. God is not so concerned with the words as He is with the attitude of your heart.

Dear Father,

I admit that I have sinned. I believe that the Lord Jesus Christ died for me and paid for my sins. I am now, by an act of faith, putting all my trust in Jesus Christ alone to forgive my sins, come into my life, and give me eternal life. Thank you for doing all this as you promised.

Does that prayer express the desire of your heart? If it does, pray that prayer right now, and Christ will come into your life, as He promised.

God promised that if you received Christ by faith, you would become a child of God (see John 1:12). Would God ever mislead you? On what authority do you know that God has answered your prayer? (The trustworthiness of God and His Word).

WHERE DO WE GO FROM HERE?

Now that you have trusted Christ as your Savior, are you sure you would go to heaven if you were to die tonight? If you were to die tonight and come before God and He asked, "Why should I let you into My heaven?" what would you say?

These things I have written to you who believe in the name of the Son of God, in order that you may know that you have eternal life. (1 John 5:13 NAS)

Does that verse say you may hope or think or wish that you have eternal life? What does it say? What does it say is the only thing you have to do to receive eternal life?

For more information:

Vernon P. Harms
PO Box 4324
Sunriver, OR 97707
(541) 593-8311
(Summer address)

1723 W. Placita Peseta
Green Valley, AZ 85614
(520) 625-3664
(Winter address)

E-mail: vpharms@juno.com

FOR A PERSONALLY AUTO-
GRAPHED COPY & FAST SERVICE
- ORDER DIRECTLY FROM THE
AUTHOR USING EITHER ADDRESS
ABOVE. THANK YOU!

To order additional copies of

Kick the Tires and
Light the Fires

send $12.95 plus $4.95 shipping and handling to

Books, Etc.
PO Box 1406
Mukilteo, WA 98275

or have your credit card ready and call

(800) 917-BOOK